Y0-BZD-567

© 1989 Franklin Watts

First published in the USA by
Franklin Watts Inc
387 Park Avenue South
New York
NY 10016

US ISBN: 0-531-10725-6
Library of Congress Catalog
Card Number 89-31969

Printed in Belgium

Series Editor
Norman Barrett

Designed by
K and Co.

Photographs by
Action Plus

Technical Consultant
Richard Francis

Safety note
BMX bicycle riding can be
dangerous. Always ride with
a helmet and other
recommended safety
equipment.

The Picture World of

BMX

R.J. Stephen

CONTENTS

Franklin Watts

London • New York • Sydney • Toronto

Introduction

People ride BMX bikes in races or other competitions or just for fun.

BMX bikes are tougher than most other bikes and have smaller tires. They are built for racing over a bumpy course or for performing tricks.

Bigger versions of BMX bikes, called mountain bikes, are used for touring rough country.

▽ Boys and girls of all ages take part in BMX racing.

▷ Mountain bikes are bigger versions of BMX bikes. They have other differences, too, and are built for touring rough country.

◁ Displays of tricks and balances are called freestyle. Riders shoot up into the air from ramps and perform skillful turns before landing.

7

The bikes

BMX racing bikes have knobby tires, which give them good grip on loose surfaces. Parts of the frame are padded for extra safety.

Bikes used for freestyle displays sometimes have "mag" type wheels. These have five wide spokes, which are built in one unit with the rim and the hub. They are made from a plastics like material.

▽ The frame of a racing BMX bike is usually made of strong steel, with padding to protect riders during racing. There is only one gear, but this can be changed by fitting a different chain-ring. The pedals are studded for extra grip.

◁ Freestyle bikes are built for looks as well as strength and easy maneuvering. Their mag wheels help to absorb the shock on landing from a height.

▷ Working on a mountain bike. These bikes are really tough. They are made for riding long distances on all kinds of rough, rocky, muddy or wet surfaces.

The riders

BMX riders must be well protected. They wear special safety helmets and guards for face and elbows. Their bodies and limbs are covered with padding, under or over their long-sleeved tops and racepants.

△ A BMX helmet with mouth, chin and nose guard and a visor attached to protect the eyes. Some riders prefer not to use visors because they obstruct their vision.

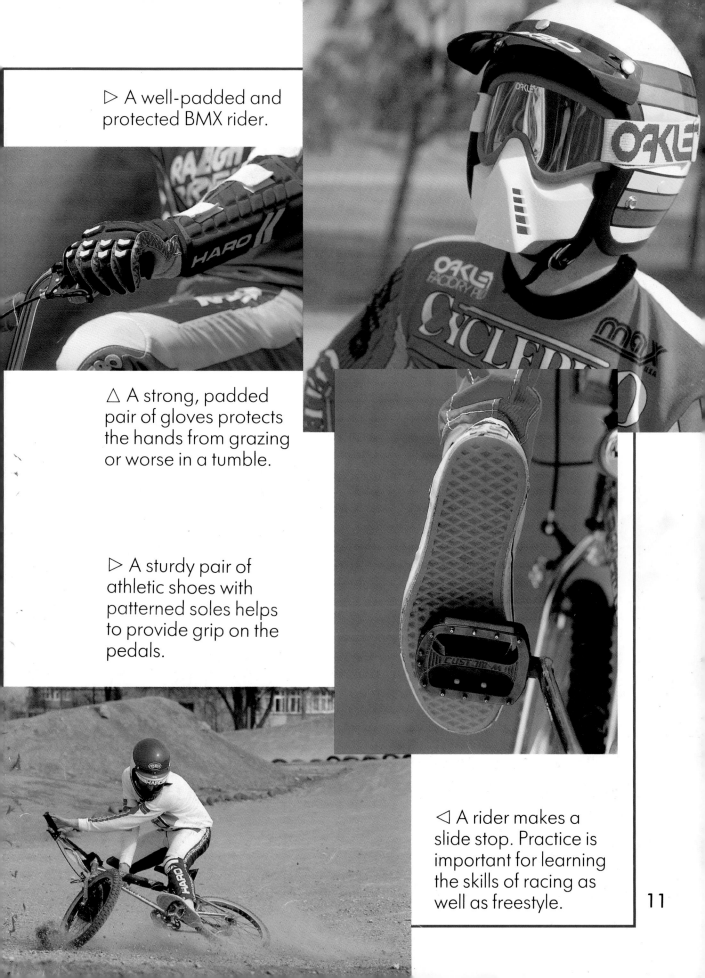

▷ A well-padded and protected BMX rider.

△ A strong, padded pair of gloves protects the hands from grazing or worse in a tumble.

▷ A sturdy pair of athletic shoes with patterned soles helps to provide grip on the pedals.

◁ A rider makes a slide stop. Practice is important for learning the skills of racing as well as freestyle.

11

Racing

BMX races are for up to eight riders. They tackle a winding course laid out to include slopes, bumps, jumps and steep or sharp turns. Tactics and trackcraft are as important as speed and skill in BMX racing.

Races are called "motos". Each rider takes part in a series of motos. The most successful riders go through to the next round of motos.

▽ Riders collect in the area behind the start, where they await their turn to race.

△ Riders race down the starting slope in lanes. They aim to be in front at the first turn.

▷ At the start of a race, riders line up with their front wheels against a starting gate. As soon as the gate snaps down, they are off.

△ Riding a series of closely spaced bumps known as a "whoops" calls for skill and control.

◁ The riders are strung out as they come down a steep part of the course into a left-hand turn.

▷ Riders become airborne as they take whoops at speed.

△ Banked (sloped) turns are called "berms." These can be ridden at speed, and provide good chances to pass slower riders.

▷ A rider hurtles over a speed jump. Speed jumps are small bumps that can be ridden fast, with little reduction in speed.

◁ BMX racing also takes place indoors.

▷ Physical contact is not permitted in BMX racing, but crashes sometimes occur. With all the protective equipment, injuries can usually be prevented or limited to a few bruises.

Freestyle

Freestyle takes the form of displays or competition. Riders go through prepared routines, which include tricks, movements and balances. Steep ramps are used for some of the tricks.

△ A freestyle expert shoots skyward, feet off the pedals, but in full control of his bike. Such mid-air stunts are called "aerials."

▷ Balancing or riding on the back wheel is called a "wheelie." A front-wheel balance is an "endo."

◁ Freestyle bikes need very strong frames to survive balances like this.

▷ Curved ramps called quarter-pipes give a freestyler extra height.

◁ Swiveling around at the top of the ramp and coming back down again is a standard freestyle routine called a kick-turn.

◁ A gymnast would be proud of the control shown in this freestyle balance.

▷ Judges award marks in freestyle competition. They look for control, good skills and originality of tricks and routines.

21

Mountain bikes

Mountain bikes have become very popular in recent years for touring. They are sturdy bikes built for endurance.

With these bikes, tourists can get off the beaten track and explore parts of the land unsuitable for other kinds of bikes and beyond the reach of cars.

△ High up in the hills a mountain biker tackles terrain off the regular cycling paths.

◁ The mountain bike is like a mechanical horse – and it does not get tired. Even streams can be crossed on these tough machines.

▷ A whole new world is there for mountain bikers, ranging far and wide on land normally enjoyed only on foot or horseback.

◁ When a new type of bike becomes popular, people always want to race on it. Mountain bikes are no exception. Races are organized in many places.

▷ Mountain bikes are used in towns, too. This colourful rider, with bike to match, is using his for his job as a courier.

▷ In mountain bike racing, it is sometimes easier to pick up your bike and run with it.

24

Flags

Officials called marshals use colored flags for signaling. Yellow is to warn riders of possible danger, red is to stop or hold up a race. A black flag means a rider is disqualified. A black and white chequered flag signals the finish of the race.

△ A marshal uses a red flag to hold up the start of a race while the track is cleared.

Winning a big event

The biggest race meets have thousands of entrants. There are events for riders of various ages, from five or six years old upward.

Riders in each class take part in a series of "motos." Each group of eight rides in three motos against each other, scoring 1 point for a win, 2 for second place, down to 8 for coming in last. The four riders with the fewest points after their three motos go on to the next round. The series of motos might continue for more than one round. The last eight left in the class fight out the final, or "main." This may be a series of three motos, or a single, "sudden death" race.

△ Trophies galore await the successful riders in the various age groups at a big event.

Track size

BMX tracks range from about 200 to 350 meters (220 to 380 yards) in length. Races take from about a half a minute to a minute to complete.

The race is started from a small hill. The course is 8 meters (26 ft) wide at the start, but narrows to 3 m (10 ft) in places. Riders must stay in their lanes for the first 15 m (50 ft).

△ Riders must keep to their lanes for the first 15 meters (50 ft) of a race.

The birth of BMX

BMX started in California, in the early 1970s. It was modeled on the cross-country motorcycle sport of moto-cross. The letters BMX stand for Bicycle Moto-Cross.

A new sport

Mountain biking also began in California, in the late 1970s. It became very popular in the 1980s, and developed into a new sport as well as a leisure activity.

△ Parents are allowed to help very young riders to get in the correct starting position.

International racing

A world ruling body for BMX was formed in 1981, called the International BMX Federation. The first BMX world championships were held in Daytona, Florida, in 1982.

Glossary

Aerial
A mid-air stunt performed with the help of a ramp.

Berm
A banked, or sloped, turn on the racing track.

Endo
A balance on the front wheel in freestyle or a head-over-handlebars crash in racing.

Freestyle
The branch of BMX in which routines and tricks are performed.

Kick-turn
A freestyle trick in which the rider turns completely around at the top of the ramp.

Mag wheels
Wheels in which the spokes, rim and hub are made in one part.

Main
The final race of a competition.

Marshals
Race officials who supervise and control the racing, and ensure that all the proper safety precautions are taken.

Moto
A qualifying race or a heat.

Mountain bike
A tough, sturdy bike designed for touring in hilly country or on any rough terrain.

Quarter-pipe
A curved ramp used for gaining height when performing aerials.

Wheelie
Riders perform a wheelie by balancing or riding on just the rear wheel.

Whoops
Closely spaced bumps on a racing course.

Index

PRINTED IN BELGIUM BY
proost
INTERNATIONAL BOOK PRODUCTION

11

796.6
Ste Stephen, R.J.

AUTHOR

TITLE Picture World of
BMX

DATE DUE	BORROWER'S NAME	ROOM NUMBER
De.14	Nelsen	
12-21	Brian	4V
10-41	Seann H	4V
01-	Butka	1-W
03-Smith		12-B
0-4	C.Fo	
0-5		

A924

796.6   Stephen, R. J
Ste

Picture World of
BMX

Herbertsville School Library
2282 Lanes Mill Road
Brick, New Jersey 08724

1112